Guinea Pig Education
2 Cobs Way
New Haw, Addlestone
Surrey
KT15 3AF
Tel: 01932 336553
Website: www.guineapigeducation.co.uk

© Copyright 2013

NO part of this publication may be reproduced, stored or copied for commercial purposes and profit without the prior written permission of the publishers.

ISBN: 978-1-907733-18-5

Written by: Adele Seviour
Edited by: Sally and Amanda Jones
Graphic Design and Illustrations by: Annalisa Jones

For

Rebecca, Joshua, Michelle, Kristina, Nicole, Fleur, Tyler and Harlyn

The tabby cat, with his dark markings, spots or stripes on a paler background, is the oldest known domestic cat (Felis catus).

On this his first visit, back in time to a Roman villa, Horace is lucky as the Romans liked cats.

Horace was dozing on the garden wall in the sun, when his whiskers twitched and he knew he must prepare for take off. He activated his i-collar. His whiskers twitched again, and before he knew it, he was hurtling through space, back, back in time, to a distant land. For Horace was a MAGIC cat. He was a time traveller.

Before Horace could count to ten, he had landed on a rich sea of colour. It was a soft bed, with a cover of gold, ivory, and tortoiseshell. His new mistress, Claudia, stroked his grey and white tabby coat, that rippled like grey and white waves, as she called to her slave girl, "Lucia, bring me my yellow palla." The slave girl came running over and helped her into a yellow, silk dress.

In what distant time had he landed?
It was Rome in 358 A.D. He was in a Roman villa.

When Lucia walked down the corridor, Horace followed her, but the floor felt odd under his little grey paws. He was walking on tiles - diamonds and squares. The yellow and white tiles were arranged in a repeated pattern that sent his furry head spinning. He had never seen a floor like this before.

Tap! tap! tap! Lucia knocked on a door. "Salvete amice," she called cheerfully to Gaufridus, Carolus and Olivarus who were working in the room.

Horace peered round the door cautiously, pawing the diamond-patterned doormat. He thought, "What are they doing in here? I must find out," He activated his i-collar, programming in 358 AD, a Roman villa, the home of Marcus and Claudia. It spoke to him quietly in cat language:

"These men are mosaicists from Europe and they are decorating the side room for the family with a new mosaic called Winter."

The men were indeed working on a mosaic. Round the edge it had a pattern, with swirls, squares and triangles. In the middle, a figure held a bare winter twig. Horace called it 'The Winter Room'. It felt warm, it felt cosy, as if warm air was coming up from the floor. He thought, "Surely the Romans did not have under floor central heating?" Horace decided, he would definitely return to this room.

Horace peered round another open door. This was a blue room, (the triclinium). It had a cool feeling and he sniffed round it. Water seemed to be coming from a fountain, (a piscina). He licked up some of the cool droplets of water on his tongue.

Horace cast his eyes around the room. There were some mosaics, with pictures of dancing girls wearing floating veils. There were three low couches covered in blankets, with intricately decorated end supports carved in wood and ivory. There was a low table. He thought, "It must be a rich man's house."

At this moment, Horace's nose caught a scent. Yum Yum! It was coming from the next room. He followed his nose and pushed open the door of the culina with his paw. There was a blazing charcoal stove lit on the back wall, to smoke, grill or spit roast food. Horace turned on his i-collar to find out about this oven:

"Baking was done in the dome shaped oven," it said. "A fire was lit inside the oven and it was raked out when it was hot enough. The food was put inside to cook and the entrance sealed."

He thought, "What else can I see in this Roman kitchen?" There were pans hanging on hooks: frying pans (called fretale), shallow saucepans (called patellas) and deeper pans (called patvias). There were baskets full of yummy vegetables, succulent meat and tasty olives. Horace couldn't resist a sniff and pushed his nose up to a container marked 'vinegar'. He took a lick, but then... he leapt back in horror. It was so sour. He turned on his i-collar and typed in vinegar. "Vinegar," it said, "was used in sauces and dressings. It was made from reject wine and was given to soldiers as a sharp refreshing drink. "Yuk," thought Horace, "rather them than me."

At that moment, a Roman slave, who was preparing a meal, noticed him. "Hello puss," he exclaimed in surprise, "try one of our favourite Roman recipes." "Delicious!" miaowed Horace, licking out the shell of an oyster.

The cat's sensitive nose picked up a sweet smelling scent; like an orchard on a summer's day. The smell led him to some storerooms. Slaves were collecting juicy apples that had been grown on the farm. What a store there was! He turned on his i-collar, to find out about Roman storerooms.

"In a Roman storeroom, you will find storage jars filled with olives from Italy and wines from France," it said. "You will see sheep hides and wool that is waiting to be woven into blankets and cloaks. The third storeroom has tools used on the farm, including iron tipped spades, rakes, scythes, chisels, draw knives and carpenters planes."

THEN HORACE SAW THE SMOKE! It was thick, black, choking smoke and he sensed danger immediately. He thought, "Is the house on fire?" But... when Horace peered into the next open door, he saw a man who wore a leather apron over his tunic and held a huge pair of tongs. He was working at a blazing furnace. "Hello," he said in a deep voice, turning to show a blackened face. Horace backed away. He turned, he jumped and he leapt - over the spades, the sickles and the garden rakes that were strewn all over the floor, and he did not look back until he had reached the safety of the door.

Scared out of his wits, he hid in a very small room. He cowered long and low on a brick bench with a hole in the top. He turned on his i-collar and listened.

"The slave will come in and place fresh sticks, sponges and water here, for people to use when they go to the..."

He thought, "Yuk! Is this the toilet?"

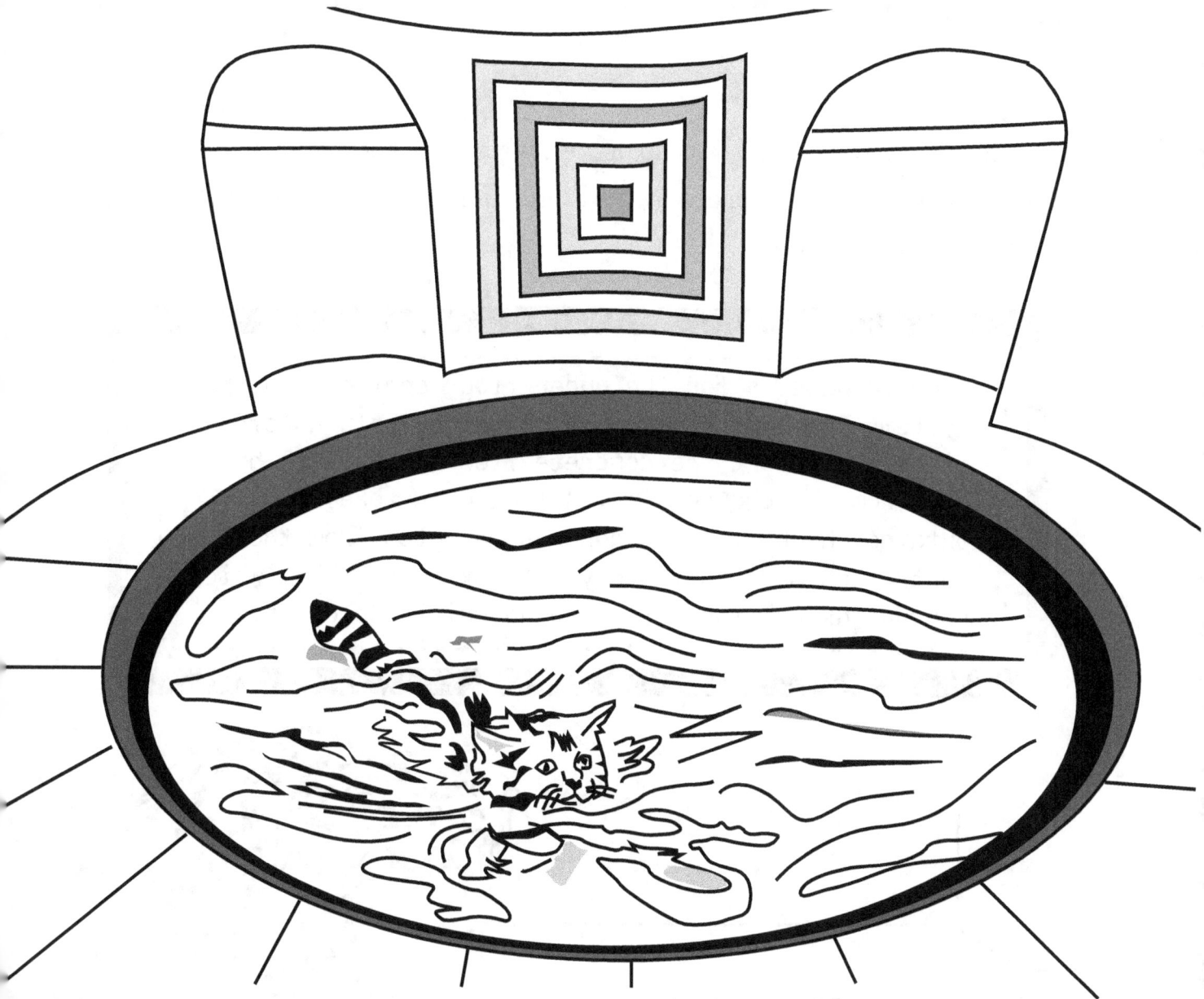

"Which way to the bathrooms?" he thought, "I need somewhere to clean my fur. Shall I go to the apodytenuim, with its mosaic of dolphins? Shall I go to the tepidarium, but maybe it will be too warm in there? Shall I go to the coldarium, but maybe it will be a bit too boiling hot? I think I'll try the fridgearium? Help! It's freezing in here!" He padded back to the apodytenuim and sat on the red and black square slabs licking his paws, while he listened to his i-collar. It said:

> "All the people who live in this villa are allowed to use the baths. The Romans didn't use soap, and they didn't have flannels, but covered their bodies in olive oil and scraped off the grime with a metal tool called a strigil."

The next room was a good place to dry off. It was very hot and it housed a blazing furnace that was being attended by slaves. He turned on his i-collar and keyed in 'Roman furnace'. It said:

"The furnace is for the under floor central heating system. The central chamber contained columns of tiles to support the concrete floors, fed with hot air from the channel, which led to a stoke hole outside the building. Channels radiated from the central chamber until they met box-flue tiles, which ran up through the walls behind painted plaster."

Horace's head was spinning. There was so much to learn about a Roman house, but he thought, "It is warm and cosy in the Roman villa. It makes sense to have an under floor central heating system." All cats would approve of this.

Eager to explore further, Horace padded on until he came to a cosy reception room to sit in. He saw a little temple with a triangular roof, supported by a pillar on either side. He activated his i-collar. It said:

> "The little temple is called the lavarium. Look for three figures. Genius is dressed in a toga and is holding some incense. She is the protective spirit of the family. The figures on each side are called lars. They are dressed in short loose togas and hold a horn of wine for sacrifice. These are the protective spirits of the ancestors. There is also a wriggly snake and he is the protective spirit of the dwelling place."

After this, he came to a bright room, called the librarium. He thought, "this must be used for the master's study." It had paintings (frescoes) of peacocks and colourful yellow flowers. Horace jumped up to explore the marble top desk. He leapt up on to the fine wooden cupboard and stretched out on the back of the high chair (the cathedra). He sniffed the strong box that was full of money and valuables. Then he picked up a reed pen, with an ivory stylus, in his teeth and carried it along. He dragged along the pottery ink pad, which had holes with cords in it. The bronze ink box was inlaid with silver and gold pictures, telling the Roman myth of Jason going to find the golden-fleece. It was beautiful. Oh no!

It was going over.

Crash!

Desperate to get away from the scene of his crime, he hid in the lounge. He knew it must be the lounge, because it was like our living room today. There was lots of furniture: an oak cupboard, low tables, a couch to stretch out on, a stall or scamnum. There was a shelf with some toys on: a little toy house, a hoop and a game of tali or five stones. The walls of this room were really beautiful, with large circular mosaics instead of wallpaper, showing the head of a god called Venus, who was surrounded by long tailed birds and fern leaves. There were more mosaics, showing winged cupids dressed as gladiators. Their fierce expression made Horace think they knew about his misdemeanour.

By now, Horace had been all the way round the villa and he came to the last room, the dining room, (the triclinium). The dining room had smart, sliding doors like patio doors, which led to an inner courtyard. Now Horace sniffed the cool outside air and tip toed softly out, past the huge stone pillars.

In the small garden there were so many exciting smells. He rubbed his nose against a marble statue, tasted some water from the bird bath and pounced on a dragon fly. Slaves were hurrying in with trays of food. Horace thought, "Who are these people called slaves? They do all the jobs, but they are treated quite well." Horace typed 'slave' into his i-collar and listened dreamily, with one eye open and the other half closed. It said:

> "The word servant comes from servus which is Latin for slave. The vilics was a Roman slave who managed the everyday running of the farm. The vilicia was a Roman slave who worked in the house as a housekeeper. There were also field slaves, who grew corn and rye and vines. The head slave also made beer, which cost four denari in the town. Some more interesting facts: the master had to pay a corn tax or an annona to the army to feed the soldiers. Roman ladies used the froth from the beer as a moisturiser for their faces."

The Garden Farm

Now, he padded down to the fields in the villa's estates to see if he could find a tasty mouse. He thought, "It is quite interesting on a Roman farm." He noted down what he saw in his i-collar note pad:

- some sheep and a lambing enclosure,
- a cattle stall and some fodder to feed them
- a stable for twelve oxen and two rooms for a cow herd.

But there was no sign of a mouse. Perhaps a Roman cat had been there before him.

Slaves were working the land. A herdsman was looking after the animals. Horace thought, "It is his job to dry the skins of the dead animals and make leather goods for the family - shoes, belts, buckles, aprons, jugs, buckets and even harnesses for the horses."

Another slave was shearing off wool from the sheep. He thought, "This man weaves cloth to make clothes."

Yet another, was training the dogs to hunt and mind the sheep. No doubt, a few dogs would make the slaves a good dinner.

Next he came to a deep, dark hole, which went a long, long way down . He thought, "It is a well." It provides the farm with water."

He saw a team of gardeners weeding a vegetable patch. Horace thought, "It could have been the Romans who brought cabbages, parsnips, turnips, carrots and onions to Britain."

In the orchard, Horace noted further discoveries. The Romans ate the same fruits that we eat today. They grew mulberries, sweet cherries, plums and walnuts.

Then in the garden he noted down some familiar sweet smelling flowers. The air was scented with rose, violet, lilly, pansy and poppy. He thought, "The Romans like beautiful gardens with fragrant flowers. They definitely brought them to Britain."

A forester stopped his cart and stroked Horace affectionately between the ears. "Lovely Puss," he whispered gently. Horace jumped up on the cart for a free ride. He thought, "The Romans like cats a lot." Horace typed in forester to his i-collar:

> "A forester is an important man in the Roman household because he collects wood for the central heating system, (the hypocaust)."

A few moments later, Horace crouched long and low in the green grass for safety.
Buzzzzzzzzzzzzzz... Bzzzzzzzzzzzzzzzz.... Bzzzzzzzzzzzzzz.... Bzzzzzzzzzzzzzzzz....
He thought, "What ever was that? What are those slaves doing round the bee hives?
Could they be collecting honey?" Horace typed 'Roman honey' into his i-collar:
" Honey was used to sweeten food in Roman times."

Ouch, ouch... Horace sped off into the field like an Olympic athlete - to find some peace and quiet. He heard a grunt, grunt. It was a goat.

He heard a snort, snort. It was a smelly pig squelching about in wet mud.

He heard a moo of cows chewing grass contentedly.

Horace looked down at his own paws. Mud!! Yuk!! He hated getting his paws dirty.

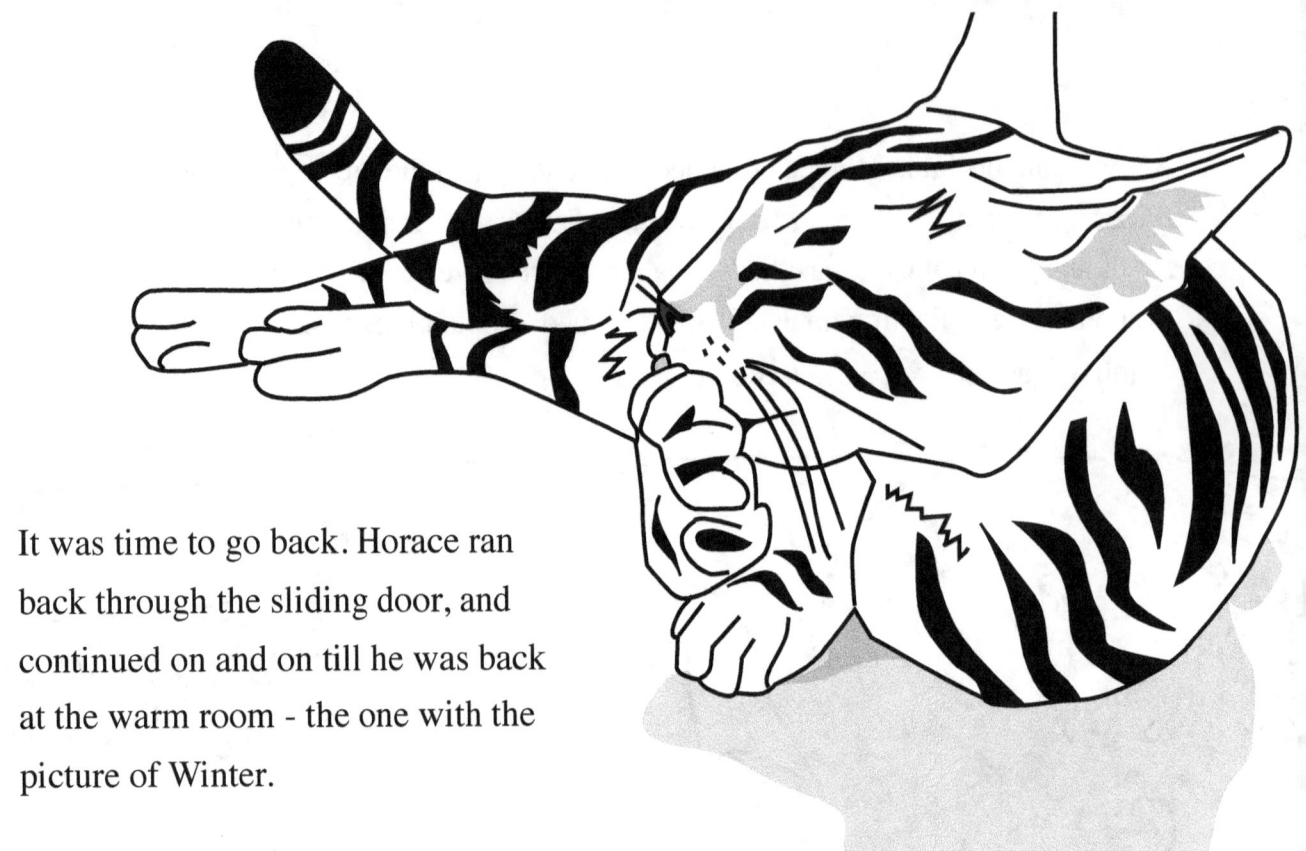

It was time to go back. Horace ran back through the sliding door, and continued on and on till he was back at the warm room - the one with the picture of Winter.

Here he was in for a real surprise. Two children, Marcus and Helen were there. They stroked him and he purred softly. A tutor came in and began to teach them arithmetic using an abacus. The children copied his work on their *tabula* (wax tablets for writing on).

Horace curled up on the stool (*scamnun*) and watched. He was thinking this was a good place to be, but then his eyes closed and when he woke up he was back on the garden wall.

Easy Reader
Exercises

Week One

> **Monday: Nouns**

A noun is the *name* of a person, place or thing.

1. Put these nouns in alphabetical order.
2. Then make up sentences using five of the words.

Horace	sun	wall	fur	whiskers
bed	slave	dress	fountain	blacksmith

....

A verb is a '*doing word*' because it is used to make a statement about a person, animal, place or thing.

> **Tuesday: Verbs**

e.g. The dog **laughed**   The dog **barked**

   The hall **echoed**   The pencil **fell** off the table.

Write out these sentences and underline the verbs.

1. The fur on his back rippled.
2. He licked the droplets of cold water.
3. Horace jumped over the spades.
4. The carpenter was mending the farm cart.
5. Horace sniffed the scented air.
6. The forester stroked Horace.
7. The cattle were eating the grass.
8. Horace peeped into the bathhouse.

WEEK 1: Easy Reader

Wednesday: **Adjectives**

The adjective *describes* the noun.

e.g.   The weather was *wet* and *foggy*.

---

1. Write the sentences and underline the adjectives.

   a. His coat looked like grey and white waves on a pond.
   b. He opened his big, round eyes.
   c. The slave put the yellow dress on her mistress.
   d. Lucia went down a long corridor.
   e. The slave put fresh sticks on the bench.
   f. The pig's field was smelly and muddy.

2. Now put your own adjectives in the sentences below.

   a. The sun shone ....
   b. It was a .... soft bed.
   c. The villa was ....
   d. It was a .... garden.
   e. Horace had .... paws.
   f. The skins made .... belts.
   g. In the bathhouse was a .... room and a .... room.
   h. .... cherries and .... apples were grown in the orchard.

WEEK 1: Easy Reader

Thursday: **Plurals**

Plurals mean *more than* one.

RULE 1: ADD 'S'

cat	wall	sun	pond
bed	corridor	Roman	spade
slave	vine		

RULE 2: ADD 'ES'

dress	mistress	bench
grass	harness	

Sentence Construction

Sentences start with a capital letter and end with a full stop. Names have capital letters.

1. horace is lucky as the Romans liked cats

2. he opened his big, round eyes

3. it was made of wood, with gold and ivory patterns on the top

4. gaufridus, carolus and olivarus were working on a mosaic

5. in the west wing he found the blacksmith

Friday: **SPELLING PATTERNS**

Put the following words in the correct boxes.

loud

cheek

bee

peel

house

meet

feet

deep

keep

green

cloud

scout

week

flour

round

ground

feed

mouth

south

count

Cheese

Fountain

WEEK 1: Easy Reader

Friday: **SPELLING PATTERNS**

DOWN

1. The opposite to north is ...
2. A colour ...
3. The pond was very ...
4. You put shoes on your ...
5. We ... on an abacus
7. We ... food

ACROSS

2. Worms live in the ...
5. A mouse likes ...
6. It lives in a hive ...
8. We bite with our ...

Easy Reader
Exercises

Week Two

Monday: **Pronouns**

A pronoun is a word used instead of a noun.

e.g. he   she   it   we   you
      they   them   ours   yours

Rewrite the sentences and change the nouns to pronouns.

1. **Horace** sat on the garden wall.
2. **The slave** put the yellow silk dress on her **mistress**.
3. **Lucia** went down a long corridor.
4. **The villa** was large.
5. **The Romans** loved oysters.
6. **The blacksmith** was at work in the west wing.
7. **The field slaves** grew corn and rye.
8. **The flower garden** was full of pansies.
9. **Wax** was used for candles.
10. **The animals** were in the fields.

Read through the story again and find the sentences below. Change the pronouns to nouns and rewrite the sentences.

1. They looked after the animals.
2. He padded back to the villa.
3. He came in and began to teach them arithmetic.
4. It was used for sweetening food.
5. He came along in his cart filled with wood.

WEEK 2: Easy Reader

Tuesday: **Punctuation**

By correct punctuation we mean the proper use of:

capital letters   commas   full stops

exclamation marks   question marks apostrophes

quotation marks

---

1. Using capital letters, full stops and question marks, punctuate the following sentences.

   a. horace was warm and cosy

   b. i wonder where i am thought horace

   c. the bees were buzzing and the goats were grunting

When you write a list, a comma is used except before and.

2. Put the commas in the list.

   a. Cabbages carrots parsnips turnips celery onions and asparagus were brought to Britain by the Romans.

   b. They also brought roses violets lilies pansies and poppies.

An exclamation mark is used after a sentence or word that expresses surprise, anger or excitement.

3. Put the exclamation marks in the following sentences.

   a. The geese cackled. What a noise they made

   b. Grunt grunt grunt There were pigs here.

   c. Tap tap tap went the hammers.

WEEK 2: Easy Reader

Wednesday: **Quotation Marks**

Quotation marks *go round* the words that are actually spoken, plus the punctuation used.

e.g.   "I will not go!" said Mary.

---

1. Use quotation marks in the following sentences. The first word in the quotation marks starts with a capital letter.

   a. The mistress ordered bring me my yellow palla.

   b. Svelte amice said Lucia to the mosaic workers.

   c. Well mewed Horace so that's where cabbages come from.

   d. Hello greeted the forester.

   e. What are you making? Horace asked the herdsmen. We are making some shoes, belts and buckles they answered.

   f. Marcus and Helena stroked Horace. This is a good place to live they said.

2. Using the story, make up some questions of your own.

WEEK 2: Easy Reader

Thursday: Spelling Patterns

Put these words in the right boxes.

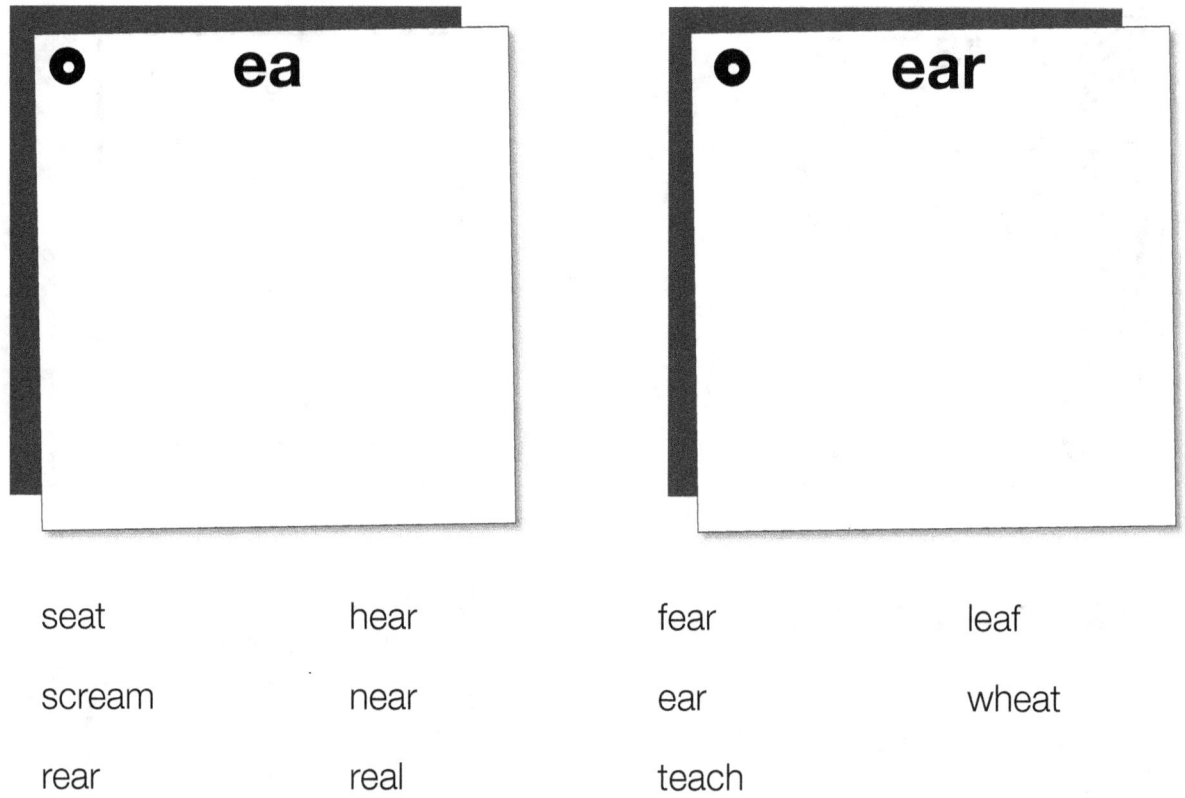

seat	hear	fear	leaf
scream	near	ear	wheat
rear	real	teach	

Put these words in the right column.

NOUNS	VERBS	ADJECTIVES

Horace	opened	big	round	went	eyes
wood	working	blacksmith	villa	exploring	long
smokey	jumped	sticks	bench	fresh	cart
mending	pretty	scented	corn	walked	smelly
honey	collecting	gold	small	sniffed	placing

WEEK 2: Easy Reader

Friday: Design a Brochure

Make your own booklet. Here are some ideas you could include.

A VISIT TO A *ROMAN* VILLA

MEET THE FAMILY.

LUCIA

MARCUS

HELENA

TUTOR

Choose a room.

Describe how a Roman room was furnished. Include furniture, mosaics and wall hangings Don't forget to draw pictures.

Make a MENU for a Roman dinner party.

starter ....

main ....

desert ....

CHOOSE A SLAVE AT WORK.

WRITE & DRAW.

e.g. blacksmith

PLAN A TOUR AROUND THE FARM.

WRITE AND DRAW WHAT YOU WILL SEE. FOLLOW THE WOODLAND TRAIL.

e.g. bees in the hive
plums in the orchard

OTHER IDEAS

ENJOY THE **BATHS**

Record some flowers never seen in England before. e.g. pansies, violets, roses

Higher Reader
Exercises

Week One

Monday: **The Noun**

A noun is the *name* of a person, animal, place or thing.

1. Read the sentences. Copy the sentences. Then make a list of all the nouns in each sentence.

    a. Horace lay in the sun on the garden wall.

    b. A slave put a yellow, silk dress on her mistress.

    c. Around the kitchen were baskets of vegetables, meat, olives and much more.

    d. In the storerooms were blankets, cloaks, spades, rakes chisels and scythes.

    e. Fresh sticks, sponges and water were placed on the bench.

    f. The central chamber contained columns of tiles to support the concrete floor.

    g. The panelled walls have frescos of bright peacocks and flowers.

    h. On the desk were reed pens, an ivory stylus and a bronze inkpot.

    i. Some of the children's toys were on the shelf, a toy house, a kite, a hoop and tali.

    j. The winter dining room had sliding doors that led to the inner courtyard.

2. Take one noun from each sentence and make up your own sentences.

WEEK 1: Higher Level

Tuesday: **Comprehension**

Read the story again and answer the questions below in complete sentences.

Remember that sentences start with a capital letter and end with a full stop.

1. Describe the mosaic carpet called 'Winter'.

2. What did Horace see in the Triclinium?

3. How was the baking done in the Culina?

4. Where did they keep the olives and wines?

5. Who was working at the furnace and what was he wearing?

6. The Romans didn't have soap and flannels, so how did they get clean?

7. What happened to Horace in the librarium?

8. What tools were used on the farm?

9. What three fruits did the Romans bring to Britain?

10. What did the slave who looked after the dogs train them for?

ALPHABETICAL ORDER

Put these Roman names used in the story in alphabetical order.

| Gaufridus | Carolus | Olivarus | Marcus |
| Helena | Lucia | | |

Now try these:

blacksmith	fresco	villa	tiles	byre
furnace	rye	plaster	tabulus	vines
well	roses	plums		

WEEK 1: Higher Level

Wednesday: Verbs

A verb may be said to be a '*doing word*' because it is used to make a statement about a person, animal, place or thing.

1. Underline the verbs in the following sentences.

   a. The bees were buzzing loudly.
   b. The chickens squawked noisily.
   c. Horace purred softly.
   d. Horace peered into the room.
   e. Horace licked the droplets of cold water.
   f. Horace opened his large, round eyes and found he was curled up on a large, soft bed.
   g. Underneath was a model of a wriggling snake.
   h. The gardeners were weeding the vegetable patch.
   i. Horace sniffed the scented air.
   j. The forester collected wood for the hypocaust.

2. Write the sentences using the correct verb.

   a. Cloth is *(wove, woven)* from wool, which has *(grown, grew)* on sheep.
   b. The tree had *(fell, fallen)* across the stream and many branches were *(broke, broken)*.
   c. By the time the sun had *(rose, risen)*, Horace was at the villa.
   d. After Horace had *(ate, eaten)* the oysters, he *(was, went)* to explore.
   e. The fresco was *(paint, painted)* by a famous artist.
   f. No sooner had he *(spoke, spoken)*, than a deer *(sprang, sprung)* into our path.
   g. A nest had *(fell, fallen)* to the ground where it had been *(blew, blown)* by the wind.
   h. After I had *(wrote, written)* on my tablet it was time for dinner.
   i. The bees *(drove, driven)* Horace into the next field.
   j. Lucia *(began, begun)* to look after the toy which she had *(gave, given)* to Marcus.

WEEK 1: Higher Level

Thursday: **Adjectives**

A word that *describes* a noun is called an adjective.

Copy these sentences and underline the adjectives.

a. His tabby coat rippled like little grey and white waves on a pond.

b. Iron tipped spades were used on the farm.

c. A scythe has a long, curved blade used for mowing.

d. Horace had a lazy stretch and went on his way.

e. On the desk was a bronze ink pot.

f. In the garden were green shrubs and stone seats.

g. The field with the pigs in was smelly and muddy.

h. Horace looked at the red, decorated clay tiles on the roofs of the villa.

i. The wooden top of the bed shone with gold, ivory and tortoise shell patterns.

j. The couches were covered with woven, woollen blankets.

Put these adjectives in your own sentences.

smoky	sliding	cool	sad
curved	tabby	grilled	painted
wooden	fresh		

A Trip Round The Farm

Solve the clues and unravel the words.

Start

There is water here...
LELW

The forester works here...
DOOW

Bread is made from this...
YER

Honey is made here...
SHIVEBESE

You get milk from these...
SOWC

You get wool from these...
PEEHS

You make wine with these...
SGREAP

These have a scent...
LILSEI   SESOR

Another vegetable...
TSARROC

A vegetable...
NIPSTUR

These go QUACK...
KUDC

Duck, Turnips, Carrots, Roses, Lillies, Grapes, Sheep, Cows, Beehives, Rye, Wood, Well

Words within words

How many words can you find within the word TEPIDARIUM?

Here are some ideas.

ate	arid	air	armpit	art
ape	amid	arm	dart	drum
dream	diet	dram	dim	dare
drip	dump	eat	edit	ear
idea	meat	mad	map	mute
made	mare	maid	met	mud
part	pad	pet	pride	prime
pram	pair	paid	pit	prim
rut	ride	rip	raid	rapid
reap	red	rid	tide	trim
trip	team	tepid	trump	tar
tied	time	treat	tripe	umpire

Higher Reader Exercises

Week Two

Monday: **Collective Nouns**

1. Copy this list into your literacy book.

   A **swarm** of bees
   A **clutch** of eggs
   A **clump** of trees
   A **herd** of cattle
   A **bunch** of grapes
   A **team** of oxen
   A **bundle** of sticks
   A **stack** of hay
   A **batch** of bread
   A **flock** of birds

2. Copy these sentences into your book and put the correct collective noun into the spaces.

   a. The slave burnt the first .... of loaves.

   b. A .... of birds flew over the villa.

   c. Lucis ate a .... of grapes.

   d. The hens laid a .... of eggs.

   e. The .... of oxen went to plough the field.

   f. The .... of cattle was waiting by the gate.

   g. Round the hive was a .... of bees.

   h. The slave took a .... of sticks to the kitchen stove.

   i. The cows were feeding from a .... of hay.

   j. The .... of trees provided some shade.

WEEK 2: Higher Level

Pronouns

A pronoun is a word that is *used instead* of a noun, such as, 'he' instead of 'Horace'.

his	it	they	he
they	she	him	themselves
them	they		

From the list above find the right pronoun. Use each pronoun only once. Write the sentences using the pronouns.

1. **Horace** is lucky.

2. **Lucia** went down a long corridor.

3. **Gaufridus, Carolus and Olivarus** were working in a side room.

4. **Horace's** nose twitched.

5. **A fire** was lit inside.

6. **Three slaves** were preparing a meal.

7. Horace found **the blacksmith** at work in the next room.

8. They covered **their bodies** with oils.

9. Some of **the children's** toys were on a low shelf.

10. **The Romans** liked cats?

WEEK 2: Higher Level

Tuesday: **Verbs - Past Tense**

The past tense can be made by **adding 'ed'**.

Change these sentences to the past tense.

| weeded | tended | walked |
| collected | jumped | worked |

1. He **was walking** on a pretty carpet.
2. Olivarus **was working** in a side room.
3. A kitchen slave **was collecting** some apples.
4. Horace **was jumping** over the spades.
5. The slaves **tend** the hypocaust.
6. The gardeners **were weeding** the vegetable patches.

Write out this list in past tense. Adding 'ed'.

- Attach
- Gather
- Peep
- Curl
- Look
- Open
- Jump
- Paint
- Turn
- Seal

Now try these. Add 'd'.

- Carve
- Shape
- Stroke
- Chase
- Rake

Change 'ing' to 'ed'

- Marking
- Mowing
- Hunting
- Scratching
- Chewing

WEEK 2: Higher Level

Sounds

Copy this list into your books.

Dogs bark	*Bees hum*	*Geese cackle*
Donkeys bray	*Ducks quack*	*Frogs croak*
Horses neigh	*Lambs bleat*	*Pigs grunt*
Owls hoot	*Hens cluck*	*Robins chirp*
Raindrops patter	*Silk rustles*	*Dishes clatter*
Stream bubbles	*Feet tramp*	*Hoofs clatter*
Mouse squeaks	*Hen cackles*	

Write the names of the creatures.

1. The .... barks.
2. The .... bleats.
3. The .... neighs.
4. The .... cackles.
5. The .... squeaks.
6. The .... hum.
7. The .... croak.
8. The .... grunt.
9. The .... chirp.
10. The .... hoot.

WEEK 2: Higher Level

Wednesday: **The conjunction**

A conjunction joins words, phrases or sentences together.

and	but	for	whereas
either/or	neither/nor	both/and	after
since	till	before	after
until	as	because	while
although	if	than	

Use the correct conjunction.

1. Horace felt warm *(and, both)* comfortable.

2. Shallow saucepans are called patellas *(but, both)* deeper pans are called patvias.

3. *(Although, because)* the walls were decorated, there wasn't a lot of furniture.

4. The main dining room had sliding doors *(whereas, because)* it led to the inner courtyard.

5. *(But, Neither)* roses *(or, nor)* violets were grown in Britain before the Romans came.

6. Houses were not centrally heated *(while, until)* the Romans came.

7. Horace didn't like swimming *(although, but)* he did like the mosaic picture of the dolphin.

Adjectives: Descriptive Writing

In your own words, using descriptive adjectives, describe the side room where Gaufridus, Carolus and Olivarus were working.

Or describe the culina (kitchen), or the masters study and heated dining room, or walking round the farm

WEEK 2: Higher Level

Thursday: **Plurals**

Change all singulars into plurals.

        e.g   Horace looked at the roof.
                  Horace looked at the roofs.

Add 's'.

1. Horace walked along the **carpet**.
2. The **slave** helped <u>her</u> mistress to dress.
3. The tabby cat with his **pattern** of dark markings on a paler background is the oldest known domestic cat.
4. He opened his large, round **eye**.
5. The **wall was** painted in grey and blue stripes.
6. Horace licked the **droplet** of water.
7. The store **room was** in the front corridor.
8. The storage **jar was** filled with olives.
9. Horace jumped over the **spade**.
10. His **whisker** twitched in the heat.

Add 'es'

1. The **dress** came in the colour yellow.
2. The **box** had toys on the top.
3. The **fox** lived in the wood.
4. The colourful **fresco** had pictures of peacocks.

WEEK 2: Higher Level

Thursday: Make a Latin Dictionary

Find at least 10 of the Latin words in the story. Make a list with their meanings.

e.g.   **ANNONA**   *corn tax*

Then put them in alphabetical order with their meanings.

Friday: Design a brochure

Make you own booklet about visiting a Roman Villa. See the Easy Reader Exercises (Friday, Week 2) for ideas. Don't forget to include drawings.

Design a brochure for a
ROMAN
Holiday Camp

Think about:

- the country side around
- the comfort – rooms, baths
- food
- the farm – animals
- servants
- walks
- see the blacksmith at work
- see the forester at work
- meet the family

ANSWERS

EASY READER EXERCISES

MONDAY: Week One

bed   blacksmith   dress   fountain   fur   Horace   slave

sun   wall   whiskers

TUESDAY: Week One

1. rippled
2. licked
3. jumped
4. mending
5. sniffed
6. stroked
7. eating
8. peeped

WEDNESDAY: Week One

1. grey, white
2. big, round
3. yellow
4. long
5. fresh
6. smelly, muddy

....

Suggestions for own adjectives.

1. brightly
2. large
3. enormous
4. pretty, flower
5. dirty, clean
6. leather
7. hot, cold
8. sweet, green

THURSDAY: Week One

cats   suns   walls   ponds   beds   corridors   Romans   spades

slaves   vines   dresses   mistresses   benches   grasses   harnesses

....

1. Horace ... .
2. He ... .
3. It ... .
4. Gaufridus, Carolus, and Olivarus ... .
5. In ... .

ANSWERS

EASY READER EXERCISES

FRIDAY: Week One

EE

| cheese | bee | feed | sheep | feet | week | peel |
| keep | meet | deep | green | cheek | | |

OU

| fountain | house | round | flour | mouse | loud | ground |
| count | cloud | mouth | south | scout | | |

CROSSWORD

Across

2. ground 5. cheese 6. bee 8. teeth

DOWN

1. south 2. green 3. deep 4. feet 5. count 7. chew

MONDAY: Week Two

1. He
2. She
3. She
4. It
5. They
6. He
7. They
8. It
9. It
10. They

....

Pronouns to Nouns

The Herdsmen   Horace   The tutor   Honey   The forester

ANSWERS

EASY READER EXERCISES

TUESDAY: Week Two

Punctuation

1. Horace was warm and cosy.
2. "I wonder where I am?" Thought Horace
3. The bees were buzzing and the goats were grunting.

Commas in lists

1. Cabbages, carrots, parsnips, turnips, celery, onions and asparagus were brought to Britain by the Romans.
2. They also brought roses, violets, lilies, pansies and poppies.

Exclamation marks

1. The geese cackled. What a noise they made!
2. Grunt! Grunt! Grunt! There were pigs here.
3. Tap! Tap! Tap! went the hammers.

WEDNESDAY: Week Two

1. The mistress ordered, "Bring me my yellow palla."
2. "Salvete amice," said Lucia to the mosaic workers.
3. "Well," mewed Horace, "so that's where our cabbages come from."
4. "Hello," greeted the forester.
5. "What are you making?" Horace asked the herdsmen.
   "We are making some shoes, belts and buckles," they answered
6. Marcus and Helena stroked Horace. He said, "This is a good place to live."

THURSDAY: Week Two

EA

| seat | leaf | real | wheat | teach | scream |

EAR

| hear | fear | near | dear | ear | rear |

Nouns

| Horace | eyes | wood | villa | blacksmith | sticks | bench |
| cart | corn | honey | | | | |

Verbs

| opened | went | working | exploring | jumped | placing | mending |
| walked | sniffed | collecting | | | | |

THURSDAY: Week Two

Adjectives

big	round	gold	long	smoky	small	fresh
pretty	scented	smelly				

HIGHER READER EXERCISES

MONDAY: Week One

1. Horace, sun, wall
2. slave, dress, mistress
3. kitchen, baskets, vegetables, meat, olives
4. rooms, blankets, cloaks, spades, rakes, chisels, scythes
5. sticks, sponges, water, bench
6. chamber, columns, tiles, floors
7. walls, frescoes, peacocks, flowers
8. desk, pens, stylus, ink pot
9. toys, shelf, house, kite, hoop, tali
10. dining room, doors, courtyard

TUESDAY: Week One

1. Gaufridas, Carolus and Olivarus were working on a large mosaic called 'Winter'. Round the edges were patterns in even swirls, squares and triangles. The head in the middle looked sad and he was holding a bare twig.
2. In the Triclinium, Horace saw painted blue walls and a fountain (Piscina). Round the fountain was a mosaic of dancing girls with floating veils. There were three low couches covered with woollen blankets from Skye with end supports carved in wood and ivory, and a large low table.
3. The food in the Culina was cooked on a raised wood or charcoal stove. It could be smoked, grilled or spit roasted. Baking was done in a dome shaped oven. A fire was lit inside then raked out when it was hot enough.
4. The olives and wines were kept in storage jars.
5. The blacksmith worked at the bowl furnace and he wore a leather apron over his tunic.
6. To get clean the Romans covered their bodies with oils and scraped the grime off with a strigil.
7. Whilst exploring the librarium, Horace knocked over the bronze ink box inlaid with silver and gold pictures, that told the Roman myth of Jason going to find the golden-fleece. It went down with a loud crash.
8. The blacksmith made spades, sickles and garden rakes.
9. The Romans brought mulberries, plums and sweet cherries.
10. The dogs were trained for hunting and to guard the sheep.

....

Carolus, Gaufridus, Helena, Lucia, Marcus, Olivarus

black smith, byre, fresco, furnace, plaster, plums, roses, rye, tabulus, tiles, wax, well, villa, vines

ANSWERS

HIGHER READER EXERCISES

WEDNESDAY: Week One

Verbs

a. The bees were **buzzing** loudly.
b. The chickens **squawked** noisily.
c. Horace **purred** softly.
d. Horace **peered** into the room.
e. Horace **licked** the droplets of cold water.
f. Horace **opened** his large, round eyes and found he was **curled** up on a large, soft bed.
g. Underneath was a model of a **wriggling** snake.
h. The gardeners were **weeding** the vegetable patch.
i. Horace **sniffed** the scented air.
j. The forester **collected** wood for the hypocaust.

Exercise 2

a. Cloth is **woven** from wool, which has **grown** on sheep.
b. The tree had **fallen** across the stream and many branches were *broken*.
c. By the time the sun had **risen**, Horace was at the villa.
d. After Horace had **eaten** the oysters, he **went** to explore.
e. The fresco was **painted** by a famous artist.
f. No sooner had he **spoken**, than a deer **sprang** into our path.
g. A nest had **fallen** to the ground where it had been **blown** by the wind.
h. After I had **written** on my tablet it was time for dinner.
i. The bees **drove** Horace into the next field.
j. Lucia **began** to look after the toy which she had **given** to Marcus.

THURSDAY: Week One

a. His **tabby** coat rippled like **little grey** and **white** waves on a pond.
b. **Iron tipped** spades were used on the farm.
c. A scythe has a **long, curved** blade used for mowing.
d. Horace had a **lazy** stretch and went on his way.
e. On the desk was a **bronze** ink pot.
f. In the garden were **green** shrubs and **stone** seats.
g. The field with the pigs in was **smelly** and **muddy**.
h. Horace looked at the **red, decorated clay** tiles on the roofs of the villa.
i. The **wooden** top of the bed shone with **gold, ivory** and **tortoise shell** patterns.
j. The couches were covered with **woven, woollen** blankets.

ANSWERS

HIGHER READER EXERCISES

MONDAY: Week Two

a. batch   b. flock   c. bunch   d. clutch   e. team

f. heard   g. swarm   h. bundle   i. stack   j. clump

Pronouns

1. He   2. She   3. They   4. His   5. It

6. They   7. Him   8. Themselves   9. Them   10. They

TUESDAY: Week Two

1. walked   2. worked   3. collected   4. jumped   5. tended

6. weeded

SOUNDS

1. DOG   2. SHEEP   3. HORSES   4. HEN   5. MOUSE

6. BEES   7. FROGS   8. PIGS   9. ROBINS   10. OWLS

WEDNESDAY: Week Two

1. and   2. but   3. although   4. because   5. neither, nor

6. until   7. but

THURSDAY: Week Two

1. carpets   2. slaves   3. patterns   4. eyes   5. walls, were

6. droplets   7. rooms, were   8. jars, were   9. spades   10. whiskers

1. dresses   2. boxes   3. foxes   4. frescoes

ANSWERS

HIGHER READER EXERCISES

THURSDAY: Week Two

LATIN WORDS

ANNONA	*CORN TAX*	**APODYTERIUM**	*CHANGING ROOM*	**COLDARIUM**	*HOT ROOM*
CULINA	*KITCHEN*	**FRESCO**	*PAINTING DONE ON WET PLASTER*	**FRETALE**	*FRYING PAN*
FRIGIDARIUM	*COLD ROOM*	**GLADIATOR**	*TRAINED FIGHTER*	**HYPOCAUST**	*UNDERFLOOR HEATING SYSTEM*
LAVARIUM	*HOUSEHOLD SHRINE*	**LIBRARIUM**	*STUDY*	**PALLA**	*DRESS*
PATELLAS	*SHALLOW SAUCEPAN*	**PATVIAS**	*DEEPER PANS*	**PISCINA**	*WATER FOUNTAIN*
SCAMNUM	*STOOL*	**SALVETE AMICE**	*HOW ARE YOU FRIENDS*	**SERVUS**	*SLAVE*
STRIGIL	*BATH SCRAPER*	**TABULA**	*WAX TABLET FOR WRITING ON*	**TALI**	*FIVE STONES*
TEPIDARIUM	*WARM ROOM*	**TRICTINIUM**	*DINING ROOM*